SIMPLY

GONE

First paperback edition, August 2023

ISBN 978-0-578-95955-9 (Paperback)

Book design by Nuno Moreira, NM DESIGN

SIMPLY
GONE

JEFFREY DIAMOND

Then, the extremities of the soul
set off the extremities of the body,
reaching toward nobody, imploring:
Please take my incipient mania
and turn it into something worthwhile.

CONTENTS

THE MARRIAGE

As in Revelation, those infernal trumpets
have finally ceased blaring.
Lovers are departing into their respective dreams.
Satiated at last, they will bother us no longer.

Stay up with me tonight, Babe.
Do not touch me. I will not touch you.
I want to *see* you.
The lovers are asleep; they will not bother us.

T H E   L I G H T

Trapped in this darkness,
when a memory arises out of nothing.
You and me walking together,
the waves washing gently across our feet.
You say something, something like,
"I feel I can learn about
the dark side of life from you."

You, the light that I can only sense,
the only sense that can be made
out of this dark side of life.
You, perhaps the only light at all,
as if you arose out of nothing.
You feel you can learn something
from me?

I only see light through you.

M Y L A D Y

My lady is not a guide
on the way to God.
Rather, God is a guide
on the way to my lady.

She is that loved wisdom
of whom it must be said:
She cannot be understood
through philosophy at all.

Sometimes, girls become men
and boys become women.
Somehow, she became me
so that I might become her.

M Y   T E T H E R

You are my tether to
a reasonable life,
without whom I would have
spiraled
into irreparable levels of
negativity.
You requested sincerity.

Even when you sensed that
I was being pulled toward
that, and away from us,
with all the inexorability of
a depression,
and all the fascination of
an abstraction—

in your brilliance,
and in your maternal tolerance,
and out of recognition of
the deep entwinement of
that negativity and my destiny,
you did the unimaginable:
you made it all safe and compatible.

THREE QUINTAINS

I

Despite all appearances to the contrary,
philosophers do not want omniscience.
The details of the concept of omniscience
are open to robust philosophical scrutiny.
It is this *scrutiny* that philosophers want.

II

Schools of philosophy are always cults.
Original philosophers make a wager that
truth is so compatible with originality
that it does not buckle under the weight
of endless definitive refutations of itself.

III

There is no such thing as overthinking;
there has only ever been underthinking.
When thought reaches its own exterior
and stays there, like a good dog, then,
slowly, surely, it all starts making sense.

THE HERO AND THE WOMAN

Woman loves only a warrior,
thought Nietzsche.
But he was not quite correct.

A warrior wins wars.
A hero saves the world.

Of the two,
the hero's path
is more precarious,
more exacting.

If given the choice
between a warrior and a hero,
a woman chooses the hero,
time
after
time.

TEATIME

I pour some hot tea.
Your prayer is ineffectual.
It bounces off my life
like two atoms in the void.

I pour you a cup.
Your love was otherwise.
It exploded my life
like two particles colliding.

MILK YOUR MADNESS

Over breakfast,
a fellow patient across the table
leaned forward,
as though to conspire to escape.
He whispered,
"Your madness is a sacred gift,"
and leaned back.
And what else was there to say?
We all knew.
The gift was not compatible with
worldly freedom.
It was not even compatible with
mental freedom.
Beyond this world and this mind,
we felt the breeze.

And so we milk our madnesses.

GOD BECOMING HUMAN

That a hefty dose of suffering should make God fully human
would be like a calculation making a computer fully intelligent.
Having been Christ, God now wants to become an average Joe.
For the easing of this surely extremely disorienting transition,
and by way of a few pointers, none of which are written in stone:
Set the table. Do the dishes. Have the need to sleep every night.
Become acclimated to the feelings of limit and dependency.
Suffer nobly, but do not display yourself exhibitionistically
with your arms outspread, as if to reach every last drop of pity.
And importantly, do not talk unkindly of your time on the cross,
because perhaps it was more significant than you currently think.
But if you are now seriously committed to becoming one of us,
do not be scared of what you are shedding of your foreknowledge.
Once settled, you may come to find new assurances at the hearth.

TEN FRAGMENTS

I

Breaking up with my soulmate,
like eating from the tree of knowledge . . .

II

Falling in love,
free-falling out of it.

III

Look how far I still am from reality,
yet I can touch it.

IV

I want to show you what I found.
"But you lost it."
Then what will happen?

V

Submission to the lady
through submission of a work.

VI

Writing as a means of moving on?

VII

I cannot dance
with only your spirit.

VIII

Let's elope, out of reach of reality;
it's the only thing holding us apart.

IX

Glimmering impressions of a world just beyond my inner life—

X

"Try to grasp the enormity of what's happening,
and then grasp my hand."

NO NAILS

The greater the faith of Love's devotee the more difficult and painful are the points he has to pass through.

—Dante, *Vita Nova*

The days would be getting warmer soon. He might have to pick a location farther north—the farther the better. This would serve two purposes. It would, of course, ensure very cold temperatures, both on land and in water. But it would also force him to commit more seriously to his plan. Plane tickets were expensive, and he did not have much expendable income, nor did he have many days he could take off from work without being fired. Ideally, he thought, he should buy tickets for a region far enough away that he would simply not be able to avoid being fired. This would really lock him into it, he thought.

But then again, he knew that his plan could involve no element of melodrama, which would include purposely getting fired. Even politely resigning would be melodramatic. Moreover—and this was the crux of the matter—he intended to survive, so he should plan on going back to work.

Of course, he knew that the time and money would not really lock him in, that if he did not carry through with his intentions, he would have wasted valuable resources, but he would still be here, and he would still be the same person that he always had been. And when it really came down to committing the act, the time and money would not be on his mind. But they served to add some pressure to the moment, which was always helpful.

A minor inconvenience arose from the fact that once he purchased the plane tickets, he could also cancel them. He would have preferred that the purchase be nonrefundable. But, then again, its refundability mirrored the option for him to back out of the act itself.

He went over the plan in his head once again. He would voluntarily travel to a body of ice water and jump into it. He would then remain treading water for as long as he possibly could. The shore would not be far away, but he would not swim toward it. If someone saw him and tried to help, he would reject their help and insist that he was a cold-water swimmer. If he was in such a mental and physical state that he was unable to pass off such a lie, then he would actively resist help. When he reached the point at which he could no longer stay above water, he would push on. The plan was to never give up, to never accept death. If he stopped, then he would die, but he had got it into his head that if he truly did not give in to death, then he would not die. He imagined that, at a certain point, when he reached the level of absolute resistance, his own body would kick in, not only saving his life but making him perfectly healthy, as if none of it had ever happened. This seemed to him to follow logically, because if a person truly did not want to die, then they would not.

And who had really faced death in this manner? Soldiers went off to fight and risk their lives, but the risk was in the context of a separate goal, so death was never confronted directly. An elderly person on their deathbed accepted death and confronted it, but they confronted it as something inevitable. Had Christ truly confronted death? He had thought that a God was going to save him; and, moreover, he had been nailed to a cross, so at the point at which he would have been expected to back down, he had not had the option to do so.

No, no one had confronted death in a total manner, and consequently no one had defeated it, so the man thought. *No one in the history of humanity had truly challenged death.*

Did he actually want to die? No, he was not suicidal. The reason he knew that he was not suicidal was because he knew that he in fact wanted the opposite: immortality. That the roads to suicide and immortality should look similar struck him as no reason to believe that they stemmed from similar motivations. Of course, he knew that if he failed, it would look like a suicide. No amount of explaining beforehand would convince anyone that it was anything other than suicide, and of course he could not talk about it. It had to be a completely solitary decision. He could not even leave a note for his family in case he failed, because such a note would detract from the mindset that he would not fail. To write a note just in case he died would amount to accepting death. No, he would not die, he thought, and consequently his plan was not in conflict with his duty to his family. His family would never hear anything about it; they would be off in a distant country. But what if he died? He would not die.

He spent the days thinking about the trip. He could already feel death, and he could feel himself making himself ill through sheer mental strain. So what, he thought, if he made himself sick now? It would be much worse once he was in the ice water. He had read about the cold shock response, which would last for about a minute and which was occasionally a cause of death, especially for people with heart or lung conditions. He had a mild lung disease, but that was just another factor with which he would have to contend. He would have to be able to control his hyperventilation, control his panic; and, if he could not, he would have to survive in spite of them. He had no idea how long it would take to defeat death, but he knew how long it generally took for hypothermia to set in, and he was prepared for that to be only a small fraction of the total time he would have to remain in the water. Of course, getting out after a certain point would amount to committing suicide, especially if there was no one else around, which was his intention. Would an impending death give him extra motivation to defeat death? Hardly, because the ordeal would still grow even more strenuous and unbearable.

Interestingly, among all his ruminations, the possibility that he would simply die no matter how severely he struggled hardly even occurred to him. He had no idea how it would happen, nor did he know how long it would take. He had reserved a hotel room for three days, because he figured it would not take any longer than that. The hotel he had booked was named Valhalla. (Despite his plan's seriousness, he was still somehow able to maintain a certain playfulness.) Sometimes he imagined that, at the end point of his struggle, he would be transported to the hotel, warm in bed and perfectly comfortable. He could then enjoy the remainder of his stay there. He would then travel home and never say a word about it.

Should he practice cold-water acclimation beforehand? Should he purchase a heavy-duty wetsuit? Should he enter into an endurance-training program? These were all ridiculous ideas, he realized. This would have nothing to do with preparation; he was attempting to approach the Eternal, and how could one possibly prepare for that? A wetsuit would only make him last longer, which was not his objective, despite the fact that he intended to last indefinitely. Cold-water acclimation would likely only make him sicker beforehand, and just as he had no pressing motivation to get healthier—what would exercise do?—he had no reason to get sicker. Because why would he do that? To make the experience shorter? Such reasoning was precisely that of a suicide. No, everything had to remain as is, and he would just have to wait.

Outside his window, very early one morning, he noticed a group of male joggers. They were wearing thin clothing. The man was still in bed with the covers over him. It was a particularly cold morning, and there was frost on the ground. He found himself thinking he was glad that he was not in their position. He would have to regain his motivation for the day; sleep had made him too complacent. But then again, what was wrong with feeling peaceful before the trip? Was stressing himself out somehow better? How was he supposed to prepare for what he imagined would be an approach to the Eternal? What should he be doing before the jump?

TEN MORE FRAGMENTS

I

Deliver me from
everything demonic about
love.

II

I cannot love
until the Christ
is out of me.

III

I feel the need to exalt you
before the real world crashes down on me.

IV

Love is the antidote to nihilism.

V

Love,
and other extreme mental states.

VI

When I cannot think,
I trust
that I still love you.

VII

She whispered to me,
"The world is our love story."

VIII

True romance, yes,
but also romantic truth!

IX

"It only works
if it isn't true,"
she once remarked.

X

The best of all possible worlds
was being with her.

E V E N Y O U

Even you fell in line with fate.
Had you always been in line?
Was your being in line fated?
I don't believe it had to be so.

I write disparagingly of love
because it's philosophically
urgent to do so. (Is this what
you had already foreseen?)

But for me to stop imagining
finding you on the other side
of this radical, necessary
critique—how could I stop?

A lingering of love, much like
a mental block, wanting you
to fall in line with *my* future,
even by shattering through it.

T A N T R U M

I don't want to write poetry anymore . . .
I don't even want to write a poem about
how I don't want to write poetry anymore
—and I am even failing at that! I give up.
That's the bottom line (and so is this).

METAPHYSICS AND
THE AVANT-GARDE

Free verse in poetry,
atonality in music,
abstraction in painting,
expressionism in dance
may be either the easiest
or the most difficult
types of artistic creation.

The vertigo of a lack of rules,
the euphoria of maximal leeway,
where the only formal constraint is

reality itself.

This may accompany either
the most ambitious of visions
or a want of proper training.

Likewise, metaphysics
may be either the easiest
or the most difficult
type of philosophical inquiry.
In fact, both metaphysics
and the artistic avant-garde
are free-form in identical ways.

S A R A H

An intervention bisects a storyline,
steepening the slope down which
snowballs snowball. Summertime.
Regular, uncanny run-ins with you,
every event becoming a catalyst,
but yours standing out, especially.
Every memory generously vivid,
but yours standing out, especially.
Eyes, nothing like hers: almost dull,
accentuating a time when it was
healthy to stare into the sun, watch
the red blasts blanket the clouds—
cultivating impressions that forever
reappear as guides through the fog.
Now summer, another summer, ends,
not having picked up where it left off,
with our run-ins. But still I reflect on
you as synecdochic for that summer,
and also on your almost-dull eyes.

THREE MORE QUINTAINS

I

The world is magical, but not magical enough.
After all, one still needs to watch one's step.
Magic is forcing the world into a new state.
One can only ever force what "feels right."
What feels right now is not magical enough.

II

The word *being* may become unbecoming,
just like any word, or any song on repeat.
It is then we must politely take our leave
and let the word dissolve into language.
Replace it with another word. That's poetry.

III

We tend to forgive the details out of fear.
We act as though our most human problems
are in fact the most shameful of problems.
Fear of the human is consoled by the inhuman,
then we become the most shameful problem.

THE UNKNOWN

Was our break also such an ebullition,
inciting your soul to inhabit my own,
to redirect me from myself before—

saving our love from another location?
Don't let anyone tell you that magic
isn't just emotion, emotion into another—

If that's so, then I owe you everything,
or at least what everything means to me,
and you know you are my everything, so—

But if we ever talk again, as human beings,
and not as gods, whose deferred marriage,
around which the Earth already revolves—

But I digress. I was saying, if we ever talk,
I would be remiss not to ask, if you know,
to point out that it has not been plain why—

why this no longer feels like a chivalric test,
why it sometimes feels like senseless torture.
Is that you talking? Is this your decision, or—

I wonder if there are mysteries in heaven.
In hell there are only unanswered questions.
The difference crumbles under the unknown . . .

A PROMISE

Heartbeat irregular,
beating out words of horror.
I'd wanted to be a philosopher
just as Anneliese Michel
wanted to be a martyr.
"Be well," she said.
I will, I promise.

AGGRESSION / THE LIGHT, PT. II

The antisocial emotion par excellence,
but also the engine behind ambition—
we all know that humanity currently itches
(and perhaps not only humanity) to witness
a prosocial, mastered *aggression* on display,
an aggression that simultaneously affirms
humanity's millennia-long moral progress
and everything lost through this progress,
everything lost of humanity's humanity
over all these millennia . . .
As the waves recede,
the bare sand is exposed.
A long, long time ago,
it had occurred to you
how lovely it would be
for your light to become
an invisible, secret _____,
alongside which my darkness
could churn with free rein,
churn free of misgivings,
churn while benefiting others.

"And what's changed?" she asks.

A storm gathers over the ocean,
so we make our way back home.

HER ABSENCE, ITS SILENCE

She holds me bound, not with a whip,
but with her absence and its silence,
and she watches me flounder unaided.
She knows something that I don't know.

Our relationship is fully dependent—
dependent upon her not reappearing
so I may complete my work by myself.
She understands how much this means.

With an amorous gesture, it'd collapse.
The slightest insinuation on her part
that it'll be all right would be a violation.
I still wait impatiently for that gesture.

For her to spark in me such utter thrall
by means of such a technique as this,
by means precisely of a nontechnique,
so I can't know if she's simply gone—

Jeffrey Diamond is a philosopher.
His website is possibleworld.best

www.ingramcontent.com/pod-product-compliance
Lightning Source LLC
Chambersburg PA
CBHW070049040426

42331CB00034B/2958